D1273765

Faith, Hope, and Love

ВЕРА, НАДЕЖДА, ЛЮБОВЬ

**Selected Scripture verses in English and Russian
with photos from Russia, Belarus,
Ukraine, and Kazakhstan**

Faith, Hope, and Love - ВЕРА, НАДЕЖДА, ЛЮБОВЬ

Editor and Principal Photographer: Timothy Dabner
Copy Editors: Robyn Whitlock, Joel Griffith; Executive Editor: Dr. Robert Provost
Contributing Editors: Tom MacAdam, Mary Alice Titcomb, Lana Yusov
Layout and Design: Timothy Dabner, Hannah Korsky
Technical Assistance: Willie Rusin

Printed in the USA - Lifetouch Production, Loves Park, Illinois

Slavic Gospel Association
6151 Commonwealth Drive, Loves Park, Illinois 61111
1-800-BIBLE-50 - www.sga.org

ISBN 978-1-56773-091-3

Celebrating SGA *75 years*

***But now faith, hope, love, abide these three;
but the greatest of these is love.***

(1 Corinthians 13:13)

Nothing is more inspirational than the purity of Scripture. This little book contains selected Scripture verses in English and in Russian, paired with photos from Russia, Belarus, Ukraine and Kazakhstan. The photos were taken on many ministry trips to the former Soviet Union over a period of 18 years since the fall of the Iron Curtain in December 1991.

As a thank you to those who have supported SGA over our 75-year history, we wanted to share this book with you. The Scripture verses support basic tenets of our faith, starting with Faith, Hope, and Love, and finishing up with Grace, Salvation, and Inspiration.

We hope you will be touched by the precious faces and inspired by the Word of God in the pages of this book. We pray that you will be blessed and moved by the work of our Savior in the lands of Russia. We also hope you will find it interesting to see the parallel Russian text juxtaposed with the English text. One interesting note is that in Psalms, the Russian Bible has the verses and chapters divided differently than the English versions. You will find that the references reflect those differences.

Thank you!

Introduction

In 1934, a Russian immigrant to America named Peter Deyneka founded Slavic Gospel Association with one burning passion — to reach the people in his beloved homeland for Christ. Under communism, Peter's opportunities in the Soviet Union were restricted, but he traveled the world getting Christians to pray for the day when it could happen, taking to heart the promise of God in Scripture . . . *'Call to Me and I will answer you, and I will tell you great and mighty things, which you do not know' (Jeremiah 33:3)*.

Peter Deyneka had undying faith in the Word of God, hope for the salvation of his Russian people, and everlasting love in his faithful God and Father. We trust that he would rejoice to see how his prayers — and the prayers of millions of others — have been answered since 1989, when communist rule began to crumble at last. It is our prayer that this little book will be a blessing and inspiration as you reflect on the promises of God's Word and glimpse the faces and places where He is continuing to build His church across the lands of Russia.

BEPA

Faith

Вера же есть осуществление ожидаемого и уверенность в невидимом.

(ЕВРЕЯМ 11:1)

Now faith is the assurance of things hoped for, the conviction of things not seen.

(Hebrews 11:1)

…but the righteous will live by his faith.
(Habakkuk 2:4)

Праведный своею верою жив будет.
(АВВАКУМА 2:4)

Делая добро, да не унываем, ибо в свое время пожнем, если не ослабеем.

(ГАЛАТАМ 6:9)

Let us not lose heart in doing good, for in due time we will reap if we do not grow weary.

(Galatians 6:9)

Trust in the Lord with all your heart and do not lean on your own understanding.

(Proverbs 3:5)

Надейся на Господа всем сердцем твоим, и не полагайся на разум твой.

(ПРИТЧЕЙ 3:5)

*Подвигом добрым я подвизался,
течение совершил, веру сохранил.*
(2-е ТИМОФЕЮ 4:7)

*I have fought the good fight, I have finished
the course, I have kept the faith.*
(2 Timothy 4:7)

For you are all sons of God through faith in Christ Jesus.

(Galatians 3:26)

Ибо все вы сыны Божии по вере во Христа Иисуса.

(ГАЛАТАМ 3:26)

Ибо мы ходим верою, а не видением.
(2-е КОРИНФЯНАМ 5:7)

for we walk by faith, not by sight.
(2 Corinthians 5:7)

*So faith comes from hearing, and hearing
by the word of Christ.*

(Romans 10:17)

**Итак вера от слышания, а слышание
от слова Божия.**

(РИМЛЯНАМ 10:17)

Благословен человек, который надеется на Господа, и которого упование–Господь.

(ИЕРЕМИИ 17:7)

Blessed is the man who trusts in the Lord and whose trust is the Lord.

(Jeremiah 17:7)

НАДЕЖДА

Hope

"For I know the plans that I have for you,"
declares the Lord, "plans for welfare and not
for calamity to give you a future and a hope."
(Jeremiah 29:11)

Ибо только я знаю намерения, какие
имею о вас, говорит Господь, намерения
во благо, а не на зло, чтобы дать вам
будущность и надежду.
(ИЕРЕМИИ 29:11)

Мужайтесь, и да укрепляется сердце ваше, все надеющиеся на Господа!

(ПСАЛОМ 30:25)

Be strong and let your heart take courage, all you who hope in the Lord.

(Psalm 31:24)

*Surely there is a future, and your hope
will not be cut off.*

(Proverbs 23:18)

**Потому что есть будущность, и
надежда твоя не потеряна.**

(ПРИТЧЕЙ 23:18)

Бог же надежды да исполнит вас всякой радости и мира в вере, дабы вы, силою Духа Святаго, обогатились надеждою.

(РИМЛЯНАМ 15:13)

Now may the God of hope fill you with all joy and peace in believing, so that you will abound in hope by the power of the Holy Spirit.

(Romans 15:13)

For I hope in You, O Lord; You will answer, O Lord my God.

(Psalm 38:15)

Ибо на Тебя, Господи, уповаю я; Ты услышишь, Господи, Боже мой.

(ПСАЛОМ 37:16)

*Да будет милость Твоя, Господи,
над нами, как мы уповаем на Тебя.*
(ПСАЛОМ 32:22)

*Let Your lovingkindness, O Lord, be upon
us, according as we have hoped in You.*
(Psalm 33:22)

*For You are my hope; O Lord God, You are
my confidence from my youth.*

(Psalm 71:5)

**Ибо Ты—надежда моя, Господи Боже,
упование мое от юности моей.**

(ПСАЛОМ 70:5)

Вот, око Господне над боящимися Его и уповающими на милость Его.

(ПСАЛОМ 32:18)

Behold, the eye of the Lord is on those who fear Him, on those who hope for His lovingkindness,

(Psalm 33:18)

ЛЮБОВЬ

_____

Love

For God so loved the world, that He gave His only begotten Son, that whoever believes in Him shall not perish, but have eternal life.

(John 3:16)

Ибо так возлюбил Бог мир, что отдал Сына Своего Единородного, дабы всякий верующий в Него, не погиб, но имел жизнь вечную.

(ИОАННА 3:16)

*Как люблю я закон Твой! весь
день размышляю о нем.*

(ПСАЛОМ 118:97)

*O how I love Your law! It is my
meditation all the day.*

(Psalm 119:97)

See how great a love the Father has bestowed on us, that we would be called children of God…

(1 John 3:1)

Смотрите, какую любовь дал нам Отец, чтобы нам называться и быть детьми Божиими.

(1-е ИОАННА 3:1)

Люби Господа, Бога твоего, всем сердцем твоим, и всею душею твоею и всеми силами твоими.
(ВТОРОЗАКОНИЕ 6:5)

You shall love the Lord your God with all your heart and with all your soul and with all your might.
(Deuteronomy 6:5)

… "I have loved you with an everlasting love;
therefore I have drawn you with lovingkindness."

(Jeremiah 31:3)

Любовью вечною я возлюбил тебя и
потому простер к тебе благоволение.

(ИЕРЕМИИ 31:3)

*Придите ко Мне все труждающиеся
и обремененные, и я успокою вас.*

(МАТФЕЯ 11:28)

*Come to Me, all who are weary and
heavy-laden, and I will give you rest.*

(Matthew 11:28)

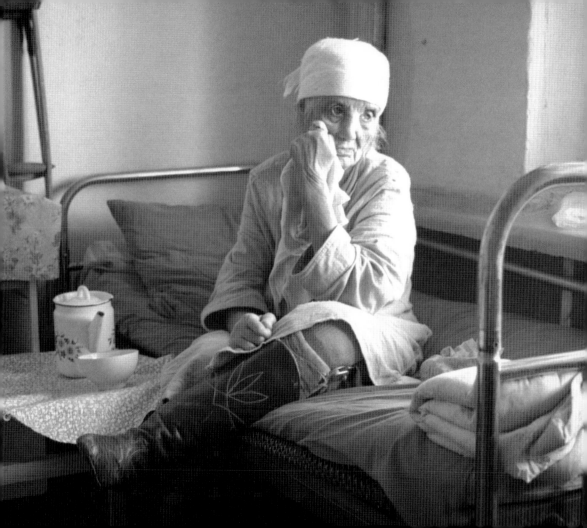

...He will exult over you with joy, He will be quiet in His love, He will rejoice over you with shouts of joy.

(Zephaniah 3:17)

Возвеселится о тебе радостью, будет милостив по любви Своей, будет торжествовать о тебе с ликованием.

(СОФОНИИ 3:17)

Буду утешаться заповедями
Твоими, которые возлюбил.
(ПСАЛОМ 118:47)

*I shall delight in Your
commandments, which I love.*
(Psalm 119:47)

Beyond all these things put on love,
which is the perfect bond of unity.

(Colossians 3:14)

Более же всего облекитесь
в любовь, которая есть
совокупность совершенства.

(КОЛОССЯНАМ 3:14)

Почитай отца и мать, и люби ближнего твоего, как самого себя.

(МАТФЕЯ 19:19)

"Honor your father and mother; and you shall love your neighbor as yourself."

(Matthew 19:19)

БЛАГОДАТЬ

_____

Grace

Hear, O Lord, and be gracious to me; O Lord, be my helper.

(Psalm 30:10)

Услышь, Господи, и помилуй меня; Господи! будь мне помощником.

(ПСАЛОМ 29:11)

Посему да приступаем с дерзновением к престолу благодати, чтобы получить милость и обрести благодать для благовременной помощи.

(ЕВРЕЯМ 4:16)

Therefore let us draw near with confidence to the throne of grace, so that we may receive mercy and find grace to help in time of need.

(Hebrews 4:16)

Every good thing given and every perfect gift is from above, coming down from the Father of lights, with whom there is no variation or shifting shadow.

(James 1:17)

Всякое даяние доброе и всякий дар совершенный нисходит свыше, от Отца светов, у Которого нет изменения и ни тени перемены.

(ИАКОВА 1:17)

Укажи мне, Господи, пути Твои и
научи меня стезям Твоим.
(ПСАЛОМ 24:4)

Make me know Your ways, O Lord;
teach me Your paths.
(Psalm 25:4)

*The name of the Lord is a strong tower; the
righteous runs into it and is safe.*

(Proverbs 18:10)

**Имя Господа–крепкая башня: убегает в
нее праведник–и безопасен.**

(ПРИТЧЕЙ 18:10)

Жизнь и милость даровал мне, и попечение Твое хранило дух мой?

(ИОВА 10:12)

You have granted me life and lovingkindness; and Your care has preserved my spirit.

(Job 10:12)

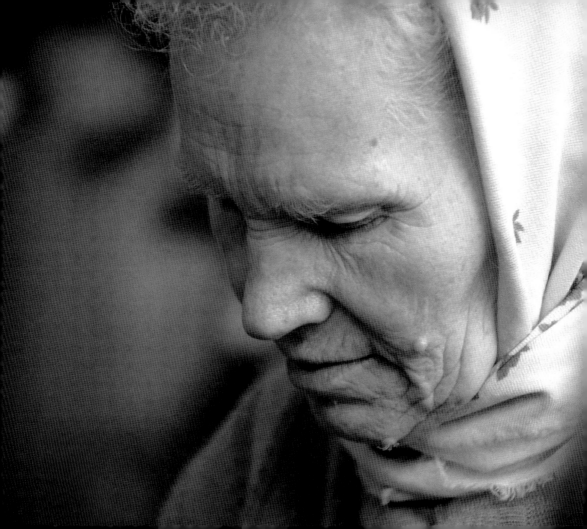

The Lord is good to all, and His mercies are over all His works.

(Psalm 145:9)

Благ Господь ко всем, и щедроты Его на всех делах Его.

(ПСАЛОМ 144:9)

Да придет ко мне милосердие Твое,
и я буду жить; ибо закон Твой–
утешение мое.

(ПСАЛОМ 118:77)

May Your compassion come to me that I
may live, for Your law is my delight.

(Psalm 119:77)

…"My grace is sufficient for you." …
(2 Corinthians 12:9)

Довольно для тебя благодати Моей.
(2-е КОРИНФЯНАМ 12:9)

СПАСЕНИЕ

Salvation

*Behold, God is my salvation, I will
trust and not be afraid; …*

(Isaiah 12:2)

**Вот, Бог–спасение мое:
уповаю на Него и не боюсь.**

(ИСАИИ 12:2)

Ибо всякий, кто призовет имя Господне, спасется.

(РИМЛЯНАМ 10:13)

..."Whoever will call on the name of the Lord will be saved."

(Romans 10:13)

Therefore there is now no condemnation
for those who are in Christ Jesus.

(Romans 8:1)

Итак нет ныне никакого осуждения
тем, которые во Христе Иисусе...

(РИМЛЯНАМ 8:1)

Да придут ко мне милости Твои, Господи,
спасение Твое по слову Твоему.

(ПСАЛОМ 118:41)

May Your lovingkindnesses also come to me, O
Lord, Your salvation according to Your word.

(Psalm 119:41)

The Lord is my strength and song, and He has become my salvation; this is my God, and I will praise Him; my father's God, and I will extol Him.

(Exodus 15:2)

Господь крепость моя и слава моя, Он был мне спасением. Он Бог мой, и прославлю Его; Бог отца моего, и превознесу Его.

(ИСХОД 15:2)

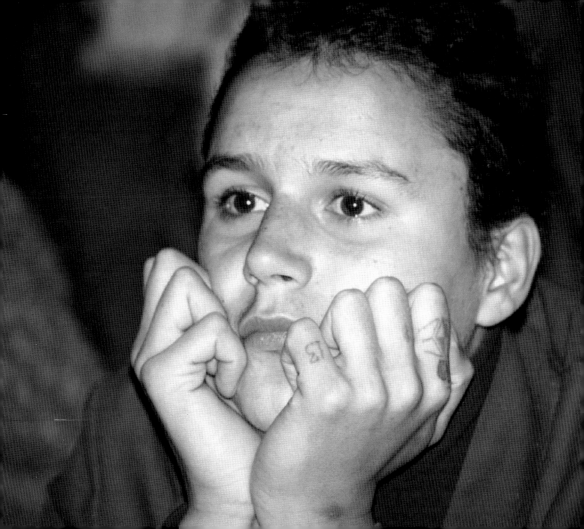

Тогда придите–и рассудим, говорит Господь. Если будут грехи ваши, как багряное,–как снег убелю.

(ИСАИИ 1:18)

"Come now, and let us reason together," says the Lord, "though your sins are as scarlet, they will be as white as snow ..."

(Isaiah 1:18)

O come, let us sing for joy to the Lord, let us shout joyfully to the rock of our salvation.

(Psalm 95:1)

Приидите, воспоем Господу, воскликнем твердыне спасения нашего.

(ПСАЛОМ 94:1)

Ибо благодатью вы спасены через
веру, и сие не от вас, Божий дар:
не от дел, чтобы никто не хвалился.
(ЕФЕСЯНАМ 2:8,9)

For by grace you have been saved
through faith; and that not of yourselves,
it is the gift of God; not as a result of
works, so that no one may boast.
(Ephesians 2:8,9)

The Lord is my light and my salvation;
whom shall I fear? ...

(Psalm 27:1)

Господь–свет мой и спасение мое:
кого мне бояться?

(ПСАЛОМ 26:1)

Посему и Бог превознес Его и дал Ему имя выше всякого имени, дабы пред именем Иисуса преклонилось всякое колено небесных, земных и преисподних, и всякий язык исповедал, что Господь Иисус Христос в славу Бога Отца.

(ФИЛИППИЙЦАМ 2: 9-11)

For this reason also, God highly exalted Him, and bestowed on Him the name which is above every name, so that at the name of Jesus every knee will bow, of those who are in heaven and on earth and under the earth, and that every tongue will confess that Jesus Christ is Lord, to the glory of God the Father.

(Philippians 2: 9-11)

ВДОХНОВЕНИЕ

Inspiration

Одного просил я у Господа, того только ищу, чтобы пребывать мне в доме Господнем во все дни жизни моей, ...

(ПСАЛОМ 26:4)

One thing I have asked from the Lord, that I shall seek: that I may dwell in the house of the Lord all the days of my life, ...

(Psalm 27:4)

...upon this rock I will build My church; and the gates of Hades will not overpower it.

(Matthew 16:18)

...и на сем камне я создам Церковь Мою, и врата ада не одолеют ее.

(МАТФЕЯ 16:18)

И когда пойду и приготовлю вам место,
приду опять и возьму вас к Себе,
чтобы и вы были, где я.
(ИОАННА 14:3)

"If I go and prepare a place for you, I will
come again and receive you to Myself, that
where I am, there you may be also."
(John 14:3)

But let all who take refuge in You be glad,
let them ever sing for joy; ...

(Psalm 5:11)

И возрадуются все уповающие на
Тебя, *вечно будут ликовать*.

(ПСАЛОМ 5:12)

И церкви утверждались верою и ежедневно увеличивались числом.

(ДЕЯНИЯ 16:5)

So the churches were being strengthened in the faith, and were increasing in number daily.

(Acts 16:5)

For I am confident of this very thing, that
He who began a good work in you will
perfect it until the day of Christ Jesus.

(Philippians 1:6)

Будучи уверен в том, что начавший
в вас доброе дело будет совершать
его даже до дня Иисуса Христа.

(ФИЛИППИЙЦАМ 1:6)

Но вы примете силу, когда сойдет на вас Дух Святый; и будете Мне свидетелями в Иерусалиме и во всей Иудее и Самарии и даже до края земли.

(ДЕЯНИЯ 1:8)

"...but you will receive power when the Holy Spirit has come upon you; and you shall be My witnesses both in Jerusalem, and in all Judea and Samaria, and even to the remotest part of the earth."

(Acts 1:8)

Much Prayer, Much Power---
and Pressing On

Peter "Dynamite" Deyneka was a man of prayer and an inspiring prayer motivator. He was legendary for his all-night prayer meetings and his encouragement for others to join him in praying for the salvation of his Russian people. In response, people all over the world prayed and, in His perfect time, God answered. The Iron Curtain came crashing down, making it possible for 500 million people to hear and respond to the life-changing Gospel of Jesus Christ.

Today, Slavic Gospel Association — the mission Peter founded — continues to help faithful evangelical churches seize every opportunity to share the Good News of Jesus Christ across Russia's 11 time zones, the other nations of the former Soviet Union, and Albania. Many have heard and have been gloriously saved. But the doors are again closing, and hearts are still waiting — and even wanting — to hear.

As Peter did, we call on you to join us in claiming Jeremiah 33:3 for our day, believing our Lord's command and promise . . . *'Call to Me and I will answer you, and I will tell you great and mighty things, which you do not know.'*

Dr. Bob Provost
President

List of Photo Locations

About the photos

For the last 17 years, it has been a great privilege to travel to the former Soviet republics of Russia, Ukraine, Belarus and Kazakhstan to take photographs and produce video programs to help encourage the ministry of our Lord and Savior in a most fascinating part of the world.

We hope your heart will be touched by the wonderful faces and blessed by the inspirational Scripture verses.

My special thanks to all who contributed to this book: initial Scripture selections by Robyn Whitlock, text by Joel Griffith, and original concept and design assistance by Hannah Korsky. A special thanks to Willie Rusin for his help and guidance. Finally, thank you to Bob Provost and Tom MacAdam for encouraging and overseeing the project.

We hope this look into these lands will help shed a new light on the work of the Gospel in a spiritually needy mission field.

Thank you,
Timothy Dabner
SGA